BUSINESS
CASH BOOKS
MADE EASY

BUSINESS
CASH BOOKS
MADE EASY

MAX PULLEN

KOGAN
PAGE

First published in 1992

Kogan Page Limited
120 Pentonville Road
London N1 9JN

© Max Pullen 1992

British Library Cataloguing in Publication Data

A CIP record for this book is available from the British Library.
ISBN 0-7494-0735-2

Typeset by Books Unlimited (Nottm) – Sutton in Ashfield, NG17 1AL
Printed and bound in Great Britain by Clays Ltd, St Ives Plc

Contents

Introduction

Every bookkeeping or accounting system is based on a cash book. It is the one book which every business must keep. The movement of money must be recorded and even the most sophisticated system requires a manually kept record at some stage. Therefore it is important to understand the purpose of a cash book and to appreciate the various methods by which it can be kept.

A well kept cash book is essential whether the rest of the bookkeeping is done manually, on a computer, or left to an accountant.

In the simplest form the cash book is just a record of receipts and payments by a business, but it is advisable to analyse both the income and the expenditure according to its source or type. This is best done as each entry is made because otherwise the details may be forgotten.

Money paid into a bank and cheques written need not be recorded in the cash book immediately provided that details of these are on the paying-in slip or the cheque counterfoil. But receipts and payments in cash are easily forgotten and should be recorded as they happen.

A good commercial stationer can supply a manual bookkeeping system which may be simply a pre-printed cash book or a more complete system including Value Added Tax records, day books and ledgers. By following the instructions you will find that such systems are usually easy to operate without much training but, before proceeding, it is wise to seek advice from a qualified accountant, who will also be needed for the completion of the annual accounts.

To employ an accountant to do all the bookkeeping work can be very expensive because he or she will have to attend to many jobs every month to make sure that the records are accurate. You will need some knowledge of accounting before you can have meaningful discussions with the accountant and get a complete understanding of your state of affairs.

A computer does not provide an automatic answer. It only does what it is told. The program will only give the right information if it is given the right data. So it is important to know how and what to tell it and also to be able to recognise whether it has processed the data correctly and come up with the right information. This requires some understanding of the functions of bookkeeping. There is a very large number of accounting packages available and you are well advised to consult an accountant before selecting the one most suited to your business.

It is a matter for each business to decide the most economical and effective bookkeeping approach according to its size and complexity. However, the cash book is the key to successful bookkeeping whichever approach you adopt. So make sure, before you decide, that you have a sound understanding of the cash book and its relation to the rest of the bookkeeping system. Without this you cannot hope to be in full control of your finances. It is your business and your living and you should not leave the financial control in someone else's hands.

The following pages describe the way to record the movement of money in the cash book and also outline how the cash book links with the other accounting books and records to provide a complete picture of the financial state of affairs of the business.

1. Why a cash book is necessary

Very often, when people get home from shopping, a day out, or even just going to work, they are surprised at how much money they have spent. What is more, they have difficulty in explaining what they have spent it on. But the amount in their purse, or their pocket, is proof that the money has been spent and that they are not as well off as they thought.

It can be the same in a business. Unless there is an accurate record of receipts and payments, money may come and go, quite out of control, and sooner or later it's 'panic stations'.

Some folk may just look at their bank statement and be content if there is a bigger balance than when they last looked. But that is not very clever, as this example shows:

> A man received his bank statement in March showing a balance of £1000.
> At the end of April his statement showed that he had a balance of £1300.
> He thinks he is £300 better off.
> The bank statement is not wrong, but like any bank statement, it is not up to date.

If he had stopped to check it he would have found that four cheques, which he had sent off a few days ago, had not yet gone through the bank. These cheques were:

Electricity	£140
Telephone	105
Road tax	100
A supplier of stock	237
	£582

So really his balance was only £718 (£1300 – £582) and he was £282 worse off than he was in March, not £300 better off, as he thought.

How much easier it would have been if he had kept a record of the amounts he had paid into the bank and of the cheques he had sent out. This would have showed him straightaway that he had £718.

It is not impossible to keep all the bank statements in a file and use them as a cash book. But it is an extremely difficult way to go about it and very time consuming.

A bank statement would be required at least each week.
It would be out of date when it arrived.
Adjustments would be needed for cheques not yet presented to the bank.
It would not tell you where money had been received from – takings, VAT refund, sales of scrap, sale of a car, a loan?
It shows cheque numbers and amounts but not who has been paid – wages, rent, stock suppliers, drawings for housekeeping, cash drawn to buy office milk and tea or to make small purchases.

The statements would have so many notes written on them that they would be almost impossible to understand.

What about the many businesses that do most of their trade in cash and seldom use their bank account? A bank statement would not be much help to them.

Yet they, of all people, have to be particularly careful. Even if they keep records, some people, including the Inland Revenue, get the idea that they might not be recording all of their receipts – some of them go straight into the proprietor's pocket, unrecorded.

It is essential for such businesses to demonstrate that they have a system of handling and recording cash which, as far as possible, guarantees its accuracy and completeness.

No one can hope to get away with records which show a small income when their lifestyle shows the opposite.

A proper cash book is the simplest of records to keep and all that is needed is what is called an 'analysis book' which can be bought at any good stationery shop.

It looks something like this when the column headings are written in:

Left-hand page – for receipts

Date	From	Total £	Takings £	Loans £	Others £	£

Right-hand page – for payments

Date	To	Total £	Stock £	Wages £	Drawing £	Others £

It is usual to need more columns on the right-hand side than on the left because payments can be analysed into more types than receipts.

Make a list of the types of receipt and the types of payment most likely to arise and find out how many columns are needed on each page. You will probably need four columns on the left and at least nine on the right. Books can be bought to suit most requirements.

This is just a simple cash book for a small business. If it was for a larger business the only difference would be that it may need more columns to provide a more extensive analysis of receipts and payments. Perhaps receipts need to be analysed between products, or between sales in different geographical areas. A larger business may have expenses which do not arise in a smaller one. Almost certainly it will need a column on each side for VAT.

If it grows to some six or seven columns on the receipts side and, maybe, up to 20 on the payments side, the book becomes clumsy.

There is another way

When an analysis book is used all the columns have to be added up at the end of each month. One also has to check that the totals of the analysis columns add across the page to equal the total in the 'total' column.

Anyone who has done this will confirm that it is not as simple as it sounds, especially when a large number of columns is involved.

Example: Cash book payments

Date	To	Total	Equip't	Lunch	Postage	Self	Petrol	Bank			
		£	£	£	£	£	£	£			
Sep 6	Cash spent	184.00	5.50	10.00	.50	150.00		18.00			
13	"	201.00		18.00		150.00	23.00	10.00			
20	"	237.50		12.00		150.00	10.00	65.50			
27	"	265.00		7.50		150.00	11.00	96.50			
		887.50	5.50	47.50	.50	600.00	44.00	190.00			

The alternative

When making a list of the types of receipts and payments, give each one a code number.

Example:

Type of expense	Code no
Repairs	402
Electricity and gas	403
Advertising	404
Travelling	405
Entertaining	406
Printing and stationery	407
Postage and telephone	408

Then, instead of 20 columns for the analysis of payments, have just one column and in it put the code number corresponding with the type of expense. It is surprising how quickly one remembers the code numbers.

Using the expense codes, all the entries have to be analysed by code number making sure that the totals for each code, added together, come to the total of the 'Total' column. Many people find this easier.

Do the same thing for receipts, giving each type a code number.

Example: Cash book payments

Date	Paid to	Total £	Code
Sept 6	Lunch	10.00	405
	New bucket	5.50	402
	Postage	50	408
	Drawings	150.00	420
	Paid into bank	18.00	630
Sept 13	Lunch	18.00	405
	Drawings	150.00	420
	Petrol	23.00	412
	Paid into bank	10.00	630
Sept 20	Lunch	12.00	405
	Drawings	150.00	420
	Petrol	10.00	412
	Paid into bank	65.50	630
Sept 27	Lunch	7.50	405
	Drawings	150.00	420
	Petrol	11.00	412
	Paid into bank	96.50	630
	Total	£887.50	

Summary of payments

Code	
402	£5.50
405	47.50
408	50
412	44.00
420	600.00
630	190.00
Total	£887.50

Keeping a cash book

The purpose of a cash book is to record all movements of money.

Money can be cash (coins and notes) or cheques (including direct debits, credit transfers, etc).

Cash is kept in a cash box. Cheques are paid into the bank.

Record

In two books:

> Cash Book – to record money put into, and money spent from, the cash box.
> Bank Book – to record money put into the bank and money withdrawn from the bank (despite its name, this is still a normal cash book).

Keep

> Copies of all invoices – (for the sale of goods or services to customers).
> All bills and receipts – (for purchases from suppliers).
> These all provide evidence that receipts and payments relate wholly to business transactions.

Analyse

> All receipts – by source, for example sales, loans, capital paid into the business by the proprietor.
> All payments – by type of expense, for example rent, telephone, wages, stock purchases.

This will allow the bookkeeper:

> To check the balance held in the cash box and in the bank.
> To show where money has come from and how it has been spent.

Reconcile (that is, agree) the bank book to bank statements to make sure that they are both correct.

Flow chart for recording the movement of money

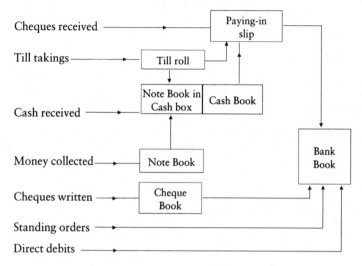

You can see how everything is eventually entered in the bank book. This is the focal point of all the recording and the heart of any bookkeeping system.

2. Handling cash

The best system for the handling and recording of cash depends upon whether most of the money is received and spent in cash (notes and coins) or in cheques.

The takings in a retail shop are mostly in cash but most of the purchases are probably paid for by cheque.

A window cleaner may have little use for a bank account. His customers will pay him in cash and the bank is only used for surplus cash which he does not want to keep in the house.

A small engineering factory probably finds that most customers pay by cheque and cheques are sent out to pay most suppliers. Cash is only used for incidental purchases.

Nearly all businesses use both cash and cheques and by far the easiest thing to do is to keep separate records for each.

Have two books – one a cash book for recording cash and the other a bank book in which to record all transactions with the bank.

Since both books will be set out in exactly the same way, it is possible to use one book by writing up the cash book in the front half and the bank book in the back half.

The cash book

Cash may be received at any time from people calling in at the shop or office, or, like the window cleaner, it may be collected during the day's travels.

Every business must have a cash box. The only exception is that for a shop the box may not be necessary if there is a till.

The cash box should be a secure, lockable metal box. The till need not be a 'state of the art' electronic machine (although that could be an advantage) but it must have a till roll.

All money received must be put into the box (or till) and a record made of its source. Money taken out must also be recorded to show why it was spent.

The easiest thing is to keep, in the cash box, a small note book in which to record the receipts and payments as they happen. Then one does not have to keep reaching for the cash book itself; this can be written up from the note book each week. This way the cash book is kept neat and tidy.

A till automatically records the money put into it and notes can be made on the till roll about money taken out.

A mobile shop may carry a till but it is not practical for a window cleaner to do so, or for that matter even a cash box. He should carry a hard-backed book – one which will not easily become dog-eared – and in it record all his takings as he receives them. If he spends money from the takings he should record this also.

When he gets home he must put the money in the cash box and, of course, enter, in the note book, the day's takings and what he has spent.

This is what a page from his book may look like:

Monday 2 Sept			£
Received: Alemouth Rd	No	2	4.00
		4	3.50
		8	4.00
		12	4.00
		14	4.50
		13	4.00
		9	4.50
		7	4.00
		3	4.00
		1	3.50
			40.00
Spent:	Lunch		2.50
	New bucket		5.50
			32.00

Similarly, a travelling salesman should carry a book if he receives money from customers during his travels. He should put the money in the cash box when he returns to his office.

His book may look like this:

Tues 5 Sept		
Alec Johnson	Invoice 1234	£17.50 cash
Grant Withy	Invoice 1107	£35.00 cheque

All money received during the day, *cash and cheques,* must be put in the cash box and recorded.

Better still, all money received during the day should be paid into the bank making sure that each amount, to the penny, is identifiable on the paying-in slip, in the bank book and on the bank statement.

This is the sort of routine that provides almost indisputable proof of the accuracy of the recording.

Cheques will have to be paid into the bank anyway, probably the same or the next day, but they should be kept safely in the cash box meanwhile.

It would be very wise, at the end of each day, to check the amount of money in the cash box and make sure that it is the same as the total receipts minus the total payments in the note book. If it is not, something is wrong with the recording and must be put right. If it is left until later it will be difficult, if not impossible, to find the mistake.

If the amount of money in the cash box is excessive it can be paid into the bank, leaving only a float. The amount banked must be written into the note book on the payments side, as 'cash banked', because money has gone out of the cash box.

This is what the cash box note book may look like:

Receipts			Payments		
Sept	2 Float brought forward	5.00	Sept	2 Lunch	2.50
	2 Takings	40.00		2 New bucket	5.50
	3 Takings	40.50		3 Lunch	2.00
	4 Takings	42.00		4 Lunch	2.50
				4 Stamps	50
	5 Takings	38.00		5 Lunch	3.00
	6 Takings	23.50		6 Housekeeping	150.00
				Cash banked	18.00
				6 Float carried forward	5.00
Totals		189.00			189.00

The till should also be counted and agreed with the till roll at the
end of each day. In this case, however, the money should be paid
into the bank each night, except for a necessary float for the
following day. The amount of the float can be written on the till
roll and deducted from the total so that the roll total then agrees
with the amount banked. The float is then put back into the till
and becomes the first recording of the next day.

Writing up the cash book

A summary has to be written into the cash book and the following
example shows the summary for the week ended 6 September and
the following three weeks making up the entries for the month of
September.

Receipts

Date		From		Total £		Takings £		Scrap £	
Sept	2	Float brought forward		5	00				
	6	Takings		184	00	184	00		
	13	"		201	00	201	00		
	20	"		237	50	237	50		
	27	"		265	00	245	00	20	00
		Totals		892	50	867	50	20	00

Payments

Date	To	Total £	Equip't £	Lunch £	Postage £	Self £	Petrol £	Bank £
Sept 6	Cash spent	184.00	5.50	10.00	.50	150.00		18.00
13	"	201.00		18.00		150.00	23.00	10.00
20	"	237.50		12.00		150.00	10.00	65.50
27	"	265.00		7.50		150.00	11.00	96.50
27	Float carried forward	5.00						
	Totals	892.50	5.50	47.50	.50	600.00	44.00	190.00

There are a few things to notice about this book:

1. The analysis columns help to illustrate where the money came from and where it went to.

2. The book shows what has happened to the cash received. For example, in the week ending 6 September, the £184.00 received was spent on lunches, a bucket, stamps and housekeeping except for £18 which was paid into the bank. The float in the cash box was left at £5.

3. The float can be any amount – whatever is thought enough to meet incidental needs. It can be increased at any time by not paying so much cash into the bank, or by drawing more out. A constant float makes it easier to balance the book because the total receipts and the total payments columns are the same amounts.
    This is called the *Imprest System*.
    Start by putting a float in the box. Then, each week, pay into the bank, or draw out, whatever amount is necessary to restore the original float. With a constant float it is easy to check the note book with box for the accuracy of the recording. At any time, the sum of money in the box, plus the payments in the note book and minus the receipts, will always give an amount equal to the amount of the float.

4. Money banked is recorded as a payment because it has gone from the cash box. (It will later be recorded as a receipt in the bank book because the money has gone into the bank.)

5. Money taken out for housekeeping (or for one's own pocket money) is also recorded as a payment. Again, money has gone from the cash box.

The cash book must reflect every movement of money into and out of the cash box.

Each month

At the end of each month, add up all the analysis columns. This shows the totals for the month analysed to types of receipts and payments.

Make sure that the totals of the analysis columns, on each side, add across to the total of the 'total' column – except for the float.

In the example, on the receipts side, takings plus scrap sales comes to £887.50. The total column is £892.50 but after deducting the float it also leaves £887.50. The same applies to the payments side where the analysis columns add up to £887.50 and the total column is also £887.50 after deducting the float of £5.00.

The receipts and payments for September can now be compared with those of earlier months to give an idea of how things are going.

A business which does not use a bank account could make a useful summary showing each month's results side by side.

Take a sheet of paper with 13 columns on it – one for each month and one for the total for the whole year – and down the left-hand side write all the types of receipts and payments. Enter each month's figures in the appropriate column and, at a glance, it can be seen how good, or bad, the current month has been. It will be easy to see if expenses are getting out of hand or whether income is falling away. Things can now be controlled.

In most businesses there will be more transactions by cheque than by cash. So the cash book will not give a complete picture. It is best not to do any summary until the bank book is written up.

3. Handling the bank account

The bank book is a record of all movement of money into and out of the bank account. Therefore it must record all cheques, standing orders, direct debits and cash transfers. Money going into the bank account is mainly that which is paid in by the business.

It will include:

Cheques received in the mail.
Money received from customers during the day – cheques and cash.
Takings in the shop till – mostly cash but some cheques.
Cash and cheques collected during the day – by a window cleaner or by a travelling salesman.
Cash accumulated in the cash box in excess of the usual float.
Credit transfers received from customers who pay their accounts by that method. Instead of sending you a cheque, your customer will have instructed his bank to transfer the money direct to your bank account. He, or your bank, should send you an advice note telling you that the payment has been made.
Credit card payments (see page 32 and Chapter 11).

Money going out of the account is mostly cheque payments made by the business.

It will include:
Cheques sent to settle suppliers' bills – whether they are sent through the post or by credit transfers.
Wages paid by cheque.

Cash drawn from the bank to replenish the cash box, for personal use or to pay wages or suppliers who prefer to be paid in cash rather than by cheque.

Standing orders. These are payments of a specified amount which you will have authorised your bank to make on certain dates – such as those to meet hire purchase commitments.

Direct debits. These are like standing orders but they differ in that you will have authorised your bank to pay whatever amount the supplier asks for each month, or each quarter, instead of a pre-determined amount. One example is bank charges and interest taken from the account by the bank, another is a supplier such as an Electricity Board, who encourage this method for the payment of their bills as they receive full payment promptly.

Keep a careful lookout for dishonoured cheques when paying in money. Sometimes a cheque which has been paid into the account is subsequently refused by the payer's bank and has to be 're-presented'.

On the statement the bank will show the original cheque as a receipt in the account and then it will appear again a few days later as a payment, thereby cancelling the receipt.

When it is re-presented to your bank (this will be done automatically by the payer's bank) it will appear again as a receipt and, hopefully, it will not be cancelled again. But if it is not accepted by the payer's bank this time it will once again appear on the statement as a payment a few days later.

This may happen two or three times until the cheque is finally honoured by the payer's bank, or until the worst happens and the cheque 'bounces'. The cheque will be returned to the business, and the customer must be pursued and every effort made to obtain settlement.

The bank should send an advice note if it is having trouble and it is important to make an amendment to the bank book to reflect the situation. Otherwise the bank book will show a false picture – receipts entered in the bank book are not, in fact, in the bank account – and the business could end up paying out money which is not there and run into difficulties with the bank.

Watch also for the standing orders and direct debits. Although they are known amounts, because they are not cheque payments, they are easily overlooked and the bank book is again incorrect – too little expenditure is recorded.

The bank *can* make mistakes, so examine bank statements carefully to make sure that they are correct.

The bank may fail to pay, or fail to stop paying, a standing order. This could cause problems with a supplier if it is not dealt with quickly.

Important things about handling the bank account

- Keep the bank book up to date and correct so that at all times an accurate balance is known (write up entries each week at least).
- Make sure that the bank statement is correct and shows the true balance in agreement with the bank book.
- Do not, knowingly, write cheques when there is not enough money in the account to meet them.
- Regularly review the expected receipts and payments so that any possible problems can be anticipated and dealt with before they become an embarrassment. On the brighter side, any funds which are likely to accumulate in excess of immediate requirements can be put into some interest-paying account.
- Maintain good relations with the bank manager.
  Let him see how the business is doing and he will have confidence in the way the business and the bank account are being handled. Communication with the bank is the key to a good relationship.

4. Paying into the bank

The bank provides paying-in slips, bank giro credit slips, or paying-in slips in a duplicate book so there is one copy for the bank and one for the business.

Front	Reverse side
Bank	
Pay-in-slip	Cheques
Teller's date stamp Date	
Paid in by	
Notes	
Coins £1	
Name of account 50p	
Silver	
Bronze _____	
Total Cash	
Account number Cheques	
(see over) _____	
Total _____	Total as overleaf _____

On the reverse side of the paying-in slip list all the cheques to be paid in showing who each is from (the 'drawer') and the amount.

Add up the total value of all the cheques. Then copy the total value of all the cheques to the box on the front of the slip.

On the front of the slip list all the cash to be paid in, broken down to notes and pound coins, 50p, silver and bronze and add up the total.

Add this total to the value of the cheques to show the total being paid in.

It is important that the amount being paid in can be identified with its source – the till, the cash box, money through the post. This provides proof that all money received has been recorded properly, and has made its way into the bank account. It is helpful to pay in the money from each source on a separate paying-in slip to make sure that they are identifiable.

When the money and the paying-in slips are handed in to the bank the counter clerk will give back the duplicate copies which will have been stamped to acknowledge the receipt. If there are too many cheques to write on the paying-in slip, they can be listed on a separate sheet of paper which can be stapled to the paying-in slip. Remember to transfer the total amount of the cheques to the front of the paying-in slip.

Now the details of the deposits can be put into the bank book and analysed to the appropriate columns, and the till roll and the cash box book marked with the amount banked from those two sources.

Writing cheques

....	BANK	................19....	42–18–76
Payee...................			
....	PAY...OR ORDER		
£	....		£
	....		**A&B TRADERS**
101765	101765	42 18 76	11223456

1. Enter the date.

2. Write the name of the payee – who is to be paid – and put a line through any spaces on the 'Pay' line and strike out the words 'or order', which hinders anyone from endorsing it payable to any other person.

3. Write the amount in words followed by the word 'only'. Then draw a line through any remaining space so that nothing else can be added. Note that when writing the amount in words it is not necessary to spell out the pence. £120.46 can be written as 'One hundred and twenty pounds 46 only ——'

4. Write the amount in figures in the box provided making sure that the words and figures agree.

5. Finally, sign the cheque.

For extra safety the cheque can be crossed 'Not transferable'. This may avoid its being cashed or paid into the wrong account if it is stolen.

Do not forget to fill in the counterfoil – the cheque stub – so that there is a record of the date, the amount of the cheque and to whom it was made out. This is very important because these details will have to be entered (possibly at a later date) in the bank book, and it is also evidence that a cheque was made out if it should happen to be lost in the post.

Some people and businesses nowadays prefer to settle their bills by credit transfer, rather than by sending cheques through the post where they might be lost or stolen. To adopt this method, write the cheque as usual and fill in a giro transfer form which is then taken to the bank who will see to the transfer of the money. A whole list of suppliers could be paid this way by using a special giro form and attaching all the cheques to it by paper clip.

At the end of each week, write up the bank book from the cheque counterfoils and analyse them to the appropriate columns. If they are written in strict numerical order it will be easier to make sure that none are missed. If a cheque has to be cancelled, because it has to be destroyed after a mistake in writing it out, or if it is 'stopped', write the cheque number in the bank book and write 'cancelled' against it.

5. Writing up the bank book

Bank receipts

Every time money is paid into the bank it must be recorded in the bank book.

Enter the details from the bank giro or paying-in slip on the 'receipts' side – the left-hand page:

The date (including the year)
From – the source of the receipt
The total amount paid in.

At the same time analyse the total across the analysis columns according to the sources of the receipts.

The sources should have been identified on the paying-in slips when they were completed.

The bank book: Receipts

Date	From	Total £	Discount £	Interest £	Debtors £	Cash sales £	Others £	VAT £

Bank payments

Every time money is paid out of the bank it must be recorded in the bank book.

Enter the details from the cheque book stubs on the 'payments' side – the right-hand page:

The date (including the year)
To – the person to whom the payment was sent
The cheque number
The total amount of the cheque.

At the same time analyse the total across the analysis columns according to the nature of the expense involved.

The cheque book stubs or the supplier's bill will show the nature of the expense.

The bank book: Payments

Date	To	Total	Discount	Interest	Creditors	Wages creditor	PAYE	Other deductions from wages	Customs and Excise	Others	VAT
		£	£	£	£	£	£	£	£	£	£

The analysis of receipts and expenses into the analysis columns is an area which may cause problems.

Alternative ways of using the analysis columns are described in Chapter 1 and shown below.

Alternative ruling for use with account codes: bank book receipts

Date	No	From	Ledger no	Discount	Debtors	Others Total	Others VAT	Others Goods	Code

Alternative ruling for use with account codes: bank book payments

Date	No	To	Ledger no	Discount	Creditors	Others			Code
						Total	VAT	Goods	

Particular attention should be given to the following rules:

1. *Cheques received from credit customers* (that is, customers who do not pay 'on the spot', but who are sent an invoice) for whom invoices have been entered in a sales book (or invoices to customers book) must be analysed to 'debtors' not to cash sales. This is because the analysis of the invoice and the VAT will have already been done in the sales book, and receipts from these customers must be matched to their invoice in the sales book.

2. *Till takings and 'cash' sales* (that is, those not made on credit terms) will be analysed to cash sales but if the business is VAT registered, the total will include the value of both the goods and the VAT. Put the goods value in the sales column and the VAT in the VAT column. Note that sales where a customer pays 'on the spot' with a cheque are still 'cash sales', despite the fact that notes and coins have not been used; 'cash' in this case means 'instant payment received', as opposed to an invoice being sent out later.

3. *Payments to credit suppliers* whose bills have been entered in the purchases book (or bills received book) must be analysed to the creditors' column and not to the type of expense because this analysis, and the separation of VAT, will have been done in the purchases book. Payments to these suppliers need to be matched to their bills in the purchases book.

4. *Payments 'over the counter'* by cheque must be analysed to the type of expense but any VAT must be separated and put in the VAT column if the business is VAT registered.

5. *Cheques to pay wages or salaries* relate only to the 'net' pay, ie after the deduction of PAYE (Pay As You Earn – income tax) and National Insurance that is paid to the Inland Revenue. This is not the full cost of an employee's wages to the business, which is made up of net pay plus all the PAYE, NI and other deductions from the gross salary, and plus the employer's National Insurance contribution. So analyse the net pay cheque to 'wages creditor' – employees are creditors of the business on account of wages earned for work done (see Chapter 11).

6. *The monthly payment to the Inland Revenue* – the cheque to pay over the deductions made from wages – must be put in the PAYE column. *Note.* If other deductions are made from wages, such as pension contributions or savings, the cheques to pay these over must be put in a column headed 'Other deductions from wages' (see Chapter 11).

Credit transfers

Watch out for customers who pay by credit transfer. They should send an advice of their payment but it may be that the receipt has to be picked up from the bank statement and then written into the bank book and analysed appropriately.

If the business pays by this method it may be that one cheque is sent to the bank with credit transfers to pay several suppliers bills from the purchase book. The cheque needs to be entered in the normal way and analysed into the creditors column but be sure that, either in the bank book or on the cheque stub, there is a note of the amounts paid to each supplier so that the relevant bills can be marked off in the purchases book.

Direct debits

Some customers agree to pay by direct debit, in which case the business, through the bank, can debit the customer's account with the amount of each invoice sent to them, after an agreed period of time (perhaps 14 days) in which the customer can query the amount. The instruction to the bank should be used as a paying-in slip and written into the bank book as a receipt.

If direct debits are accepted by suppliers for payment of their bills, their bills must be regarded as paid when the agreed period has elapsed. The appropriate entries will then be made on the payments side of the bank book as if a cheque had been sent.

Bank charges are levied by direct debit and will have to be picked up from the bank statement and written into the bank book.

Sometimes, a business may decide, or agree, to set up a direct debit to make regular payments to a supplier – a sort of budget account or, perhaps, to pay off an old debt. Remember to write these in the bank book.

Monthly payments to a finance company for hire purchases are usually made by direct debit. Finance companies may not send monthly invoices so the direct debit should be put in the 'others' column, but remember to separate any VAT and put it in the VAT column.

Ideally one should keep a record of all regular direct debits and enter them on the payments side of the bank book on the due date. Alternatively, one can wait for the bank statement, identify them and enter them in the bank book at this stage.

Switch or Connect

Under these systems, instead of writing a cheque, payments are made using a bank card (the one you would use in a cash dispensing machine), and the amount of the payment is charged immediately to your bank account. If payments are made in this way, enter the amount immediately in the bank book (and the purchases book) as if a cheque had been written. Check with the bank statement to make sure that all have been entered correctly.

Credit cards

Special entries are required when customers pay by credit card and these are explained in Chapter 11.

Discounts given and received

If a customer has been given a discount, note the amount of the discount alongside the entry for the cheque received in the bank book so that the amount of the discount, plus that of the cheque, equals the amount of the invoice marked off in the sales book.

If a discount has been received from a supplier, the value of the cheque for payment will differ from the amount of the bill which is being paid. Enter the difference (the discount) alongside the entry of the cheque in the bank book so that the amount of the discount, plus that of the cheque, equals the amount of the bill marked off in the purchases book.

Interest on overdue accounts

Some businesses charge their customers interest if invoices are not paid by the due date. Similarly, some suppliers charge interest if their bills are paid late. In either instance, the cheque received or paid will differ in amount from the invoices or bills to which they relate.

The amount of the cheque will have to be put in the total column of the bank book; in the analysis columns, put the amount of the invoice/bill in the 'debtors'/'creditors' column and the interest in a separate column. This means that the amounts in the 'debtors'/'creditors' columns will match with the amounts in the sales purchases books.

Lump sum receipts and payments

Sometimes customers pay a lump sum, not specifically related to individual invoices which have been sent to them – particularly when they have let the payment of their accounts get behind. It makes no difference to the entries in the bank book. The amount of the cheque will be analysed to 'Debtors'. The problem only arises in the sales book.

If the payments are in no way related to invoices, probably the best thing to do is to assume that the earliest dated invoices are being paid first. So mark off those which are deemed to have been paid and treat the remainder as a part-payment of the next invoice. The same situation applies in reverse if the business pays lump sum instalments towards the settlement of a supplier's bill. Assume that the earliest outstanding bills are being paid first.

Balancing the bank book

At the end of each week and at the end of each month, add up the total paid into the bank and the total paid out. The difference between the two is the amount lying as a balance in the bank.

Also add up each of the analysis columns on each page and make sure that their totals add up to the total of the 'total' column thus proving them all to be correct. Each month's total should be added up, not just individual page totals – run on from one page to the next.

Write out an analysis of the 'others' columns so that the various items can be examined. All these figures provide important information because they tell you where money has come from and where it has gone to. This makes it possible to exert some control over expenses if any of them appear to be excessive.

From knowing the balance at the bank and from an understanding of the pattern of receipts and payments during recent months, a forecast can be prepared of the likely cash flow over the coming month, or perhaps two months (see Appendix).

Bank reconciliation

There is a time delay between the writing of a cheque and its appearing on the business bank statement. Thus the bank statement is always out of date and cannot be relied upon to provide a true figure of the bank balance.

It is vital to check the bank statement against the bank book to identify those cheques which have not yet appeared and thus agree – or reconcile – the two records. There will be other differences besides unpresented cheques. As seen earlier in this chapter, there may be direct debits which have been overlooked in the bank book and perhaps some others which have not yet got through to the statement.

You should prepare a reconciliation each month on the lines of the example shown below. The balance per the bank statement *must* lead to the balance per the bank book when the reconciliation is completed. This ensures that both the bank book and the bank statement are correct and that the business understands its financial situation.

It is important to reconcile the two records precisely. It is not good enough to get them almost right. If the bank book has been carefully and accurately kept there should be no problem with the reconciliation, especially if it is done each month. If it is left for a few months it can become very difficult indeed to discover errors made in the past. *Do not leave it to your accountant or auditor to charge you for discovering and correcting your errors.*

It will be seen that the bank book is one of the most important records when it comes to preparing the accounts of the business. It provides the necessary information about sources of income and types of expenses as well as the bank balance, so it is vital that it is kept properly. It is the first thing that accountants and auditors look at.

A well kept bank book is the basis of all financial control. It makes it possible to prepare monthly statements to show how the business is progressing and point the way to actions necessary for the correction of adverse trends. Moreover, it will save considerable time and money when preparing annual accounts (see Appendix).

Example: bank reconciliation

Month .... Year ....

Balance per bank statement, date, sheet number
 	
Add
    Deposits in bank book but not on bank
    statement	

Deduct
    (Cheques in bank book but not on bank
    statement (include cheque numbers)	

BALANCE per bank book	

6. Sales and purchases on credit terms

Granting credit to customers – allowing them time to pay their invoices – is like lending them money. A record must be kept of the money owed to the business because of such credit allowed.

The cash and bank books do not reveal this information. It is necessary to keep a sales ledger book, sometimes called a 'debtors' book or an 'invoices to customers' book.

Conversely, being granted credit by suppliers – being allowed time to pay bills – is like borrowing money from them. A record must be kept of the money owed by the business on account of such credit.

Again, the cash and bank books do not reveal this information. It is necessary to keep a purchases ledger book, sometimes called a 'creditors' book, a 'bills to pay' book, or the bought ledger.

These two books draw attention to money owed to and owed by the business. This is their principal function. At the same time, because they provide additional analysis columns, they make the keeping of the cash and bank books not just easier, but more informative as more detailed analysis can be done.

The bank book may show that there is £10,000 in the bank. This may seem healthy at first sight, but it is not if a business has only £5,000 owed to it but has pressing debts of £20,000 to pay – it does not have enough money to pay its debts.

That's how important it is to keep sales and purchases books to support the cash and bank books – they will show this information.

Sales book

Date	Invoice To	No	Total £	VAT £	Product 1 £	Product 2 £	£	£	£	£	£	Others £	Date paid	Amount paid £	Cheque /cash

Each day, list in the sales book all the invoices sent out to customers, showing:

> Date
> To – customer's name
> Invoice number
> Total amount of invoice.

Then proceed to the analysis columns.

A VAT-registered business must enter, in a separate column, the amount of VAT included in the invoice total. The remainder of the invoice equals the value of the goods or services sold and this can be analysed to columns in whatever way best suits the business – perhaps by products, or by geographical areas or by type of customer.

File the copy invoices in a 'money to collect' file in alphabetical order of customer (see Chapter 7).

When money is received, mark off the invoice by writing alongside it in the sales book the date received and whether paid by cash or cheque.

Also take the invoice itself from the 'money to collect' file and mark it 'paid' and quote the date and whether by cash or cheque.

Then refile the invoice in the 'money received' file, but this time in numerical order of the invoice number.

Discount allowed

When marking off the invoice, if the amount of the cheque differs from that of the invoice, ascertain whether it is a discount which has been allowed or, perhaps, it is only a part payment of the total amount due.

If it is a discount, remember to write the amount of the discount alongside the entry of the cheque in the bank book so that the amount of the discount, plus that of the cheque, equals the amount of the invoice.

If it is a part payment, write the amount paid alongside the invoice in the sales book. Any figure written in this column becomes a reminder that the invoice has not been fully paid. When the final payment is received the amount of the part payment can be crossed out. Remember to take these part payments into account when writing up the overdue accounts list at the end of the month.

Also remember to re-file partly paid invoices back on the 'money to collect' file (after noting on it the amount paid), because money is still owed by the customer.

Lump sum payments

Sometimes customers, particularly those who are late paying their invoices, make lump sum payments which cannot be matched directly to their outstanding invoices. They make such payments to reduce the total that they owe you.

In the absence of any better information, the best thing to do is to assume that the earliest dated invoices are being paid first. Mark off the sales book on this basis; this may leave one invoice only partly paid. This can be recorded in the sales book as above by writing against it the amount of the 'part payment' deemed to have been paid.

As with partly paid invoices, remember to put this invoice back on the 'money to collect' file (after noting on it the amount paid), because money is still owed by the customer.

Interest charged on overdue accounts

If customers are charged interest on invoices or accounts which are overdue, when the interest is received from the customer, the value of the cheque will be greater than that of the invoice. Check that it is interest, not an overpayment, and, if it is, there is no need to record the fact in the sales book. It is solely something to record in the analysis of the cheque in the bank book.

Each month add up the columns of the sales book making sure that the totals of the analysis columns add up to the total of the total column.

The total column shows the value of credit sales during the month, the VAT column shows how much of that total is due to be paid to HM Customs and Excise (who administer the VAT system) and the analysis columns show the type of sales.

Overdue accounts

Any invoices which have not been marked off are those still awaiting payment. Probably only a few of the invoices on the latest page will have been marked off because most customers will not be due to pay until the following month. But look back to previous months and make a list of all unpaid invoices. This will reveal how much money is owed to the business and by whom it is owed.

Another check is to calculate the total owed to the business at the previous month-end
Plus the total value of invoices sent out this month as shown in the sales book
Minus the amount of money received and analysed to 'debtors' in the cash and bank books
Equals the amount now owed to the business.

If this does not agree with the list made out from the sales book there is a mistake which must be found and corrected. (Quite probably an invoice has not been marked off in the sales book although it has been paid, or a receipt has not been analysed correctly in the cash or bank book, that is, it has not been analysed into the 'debtors' column but into a different one.) If the error is not corrected the books are not just wrong – they are misleading.

To do a thorough job, and give help to the process of debt collecting, when listing the unpaid invoices from the sales book, use a separate column for each month to show how long customers have owed money for the older the debt, the more urgently it should be chased for payment.

Purchases book

Date	Bill To	No	Total £	VAT £	Stock £	Rent and rates £	Insurance £	Telephone £	Heat and light £	Motor vehicle £		Others £	Date paid	Amount paid £

As bills are received from suppliers, give them a number and enter them immediately in the purchases book in numerical order showing:

Date
From – supplier's name
Consecutive number
Total amount of the bill.

Then proceed to the analysis columns.

A VAT-registered business must enter, in a separate column, the amount of VAT included in the total of the bill. The remainder of the bill equals the value of goods or services purchased and this should be analysed according to the type or nature of the expense – rent, telephone, motor vehicle expenses, insurance etc.

File the bills in a 'bills to pay' file in alphabetical order of supplier (see Chapter 7).

When the bill is paid, mark off the invoice by writing alongside it in the purchases book the date paid and whether it is paid by cash or cheque. It is helpful to put the cheque number.

Also take the bill itself from the 'bills to pay' file and mark it 'paid', quote the date and whether paid by cash or cheque (and the cheque number).

Then re-file the bill in the 'bills paid' file, but this time in consecutive number order.

Discounts received

If a supplier gives a discount for prompt payment or any other reason, the cheque being marked off in the purchases book will be less in value than the bill being paid. The amount of the discount will be shown in the bank book so that it, plus the value of the cheque, equals the amount of the bill. In the purchase book the bill will be marked off as paid in full.

If a part payment is being made, perhaps because of some query with the bill, enter the amount being paid against the bill and this will indicate that there is still money owed. Any figure in this column will have to be taken into account when preparing the accounts overdue list at the end of the month.

When the balance is paid the part payment can be crossed out.

Interest on late payments

Some suppliers may charge interest if bills are paid later than the payment terms. In this event, if the interest has to be paid, the amount of the cheque will be greater than the amount of the bill.

This makes no difference to the entry in the purchases book where the bill will just be marked off as paid. The only difference arises in the bank book where the total of the cheque will have to be analysed between 'creditors' – the amount of the bill, and 'interest' – the amount of interest paid.

Lump sum payments

For various reasons, most commonly when payments to the supplier are running late, a business may make lump sum payments to a supplier. The amount paid may bear no particular relationship to individual bills outstanding.

In this event, and in the absence of any better information, the best thing to do is to assume that the earliest outstanding bills are being paid first. Mark off the earliest bills first and treat any remaining amount as a part payment of a bill, as explained above.

Each month add up the columns of the purchases book making sure that the total of the analysis columns adds up to the total in the 'total' column.

The total column shows the total value of goods bought on credit during the month, the VAT column shows the amount recoverable from HM Customs and Excise and the analysis columns show how the money was spent.

Overdue accounts

The bills which have not been marked off are those still waiting to be paid. Probably only a few of the bills on the most recent pages will have been marked off because the business will be taking one month to pay its suppliers. Look back to previous months and make a list of all unpaid bills, including the current month. This will reveal how much money the business owes and to whom it is owed.

As another check, calculate the total owed to suppliers at the previous month-end
plus the total value of bills received during this month as shown by the total column of the purchases book
minus the money paid to suppliers during the month as shown by the 'creditors' column in the cash and bank books
equals the amount now owed by the business.

If this does not agree with the total of the list made out from the purchases book there is a mistake which must be found. (Quite probably a bill has not been marked off in the purchases book or a cheque has been wrongly analysed in the cash or bank book.)

To do a thorough job, when listing the unpaid bills from the purchases book, use a separate column for each month. This reveals how long each debt has been outstanding. It may give a warning that some suppliers, if not paid, will soon become impatient.

Alternative ruling for use with account codes

Sales book (invoices to customers, debtors)

Date	No	Customer	Ledger no	Total		VAT		Goods		Code	Paid	
											Amount	Date

Purchases book (bills received, creditors)

Date	No	Supplier	Ledger no	Total		VAT		Goods		Code	Paid	
											Amount	Date

7. The filing and cross-referencing of invoices, bills and receipts

It is important to keep a copy of all sales invoices sent out to customers, all till rolls and all invoices, bills and receipts relating to payments made. It may be necessary for the documents to be examined to prove that they relate to genuine business transactions.

There are some expenses for which one really cannot get a bill or a receipt, but every effort should be made to obtain one whenever possible.

Invoices and bills should be kept methodically so that they can be found quickly. It is recommended that they be kept in four principal files:

1. Money to collect — for unpaid sales invoices to customers
2. Money received — for sales invoices to customers who have paid
3. Bills to pay — for unpaid bills from suppliers
4. Bills paid — for bills from suppliers which have been paid.

To facilitate the cross-referencing of these documents to the sales and purchase books it is recommended that the following be adopted:

- Invoices to customers must be numbered sequentially and the numbers must be put in the sales book. Put the number on the paying-in slip also when the money is received and banked or on the till roll if paid in cash. Whenever possible, write it in the cash or bank book alongside the entry of the receipt.

- Till rolls should be dated and kept in weekly 'bundles', each of which should be marked with the week number of the year.
- All invoices or bills received from suppliers should be given a consecutive number before they are entered in the purchases book. This number should be written in the purchases book. If paid by cash, this number should also be written in the book which is kept in the cash box and, if paid by cheque, on the cheque book stub and, if possible, in the bank book.

Sales invoices to customers

Put a copy of each day's invoices on the 'money to collect' file in alphabetical order of the customer's name. If it has to be referred to before it is paid it is more likely that the customer's name is known than the invoice number.

When the money is received, write on the copy the date and the method of payment (by cash or cheque).

Re-file the copy in the 'money received' file. This time put the copy invoice in numerical order because this is the most common way to refer to them from now on. Also, being in numerical order, the file will help to account for each invoice because the numerical sequence will ultimately be complete – unpaid invoices will be obvious as missing numbers.

Till rolls

Each day, when the till is checked, write the week number and the date on the roll and file it in the 'money received' file.

If the money is paid into the bank, write the week number on the paying-in slip and, if possible, alongside the entry in the bank book.

If money is put in the cash box, write the till roll number against the entry in the book which is kept in the box and, if possible, against the entry in the cash book.

Bills received from suppliers

Give each invoice or bill a consecutive number and write this number against the entry in the purchases book.

When it is paid, write it also on the cheque book stub and, whenever possible, against the entry in the bank book. If it is paid by cash, write the number in the cash box book and, if possible, in the cash book.

Although it may seem somewhat tedious to write the reference number in many places, it will prove very helpful each time it is necessary to trace receipts and payments or to look at the originating documents.

8. Recording VAT and the VAT return

A business is required by law to register for VAT (Value Added Tax) as soon as its sales reach a prescribed level. This level is set by the government in the Budget.

A VAT-registered business must add a charge for VAT to all invoices and make a quarterly return to HM Customs and Excise showing the value of sales invoiced during the quarter and the amount of VAT charged on those invoices. This VAT charged on sales must be paid to Customs and Excise during the month following the end of the quarter. The return also requires a statement of purchases during the quarter and the amount of VAT charged by suppliers to the business on those purchases. The amount of VAT charged to the business (input VAT) can be deducted from the amount charged out to customers (output VAT) and a cheque then has to be sent to Customs and Excise for the net amount.

Retailers, who usually operate a 'cash' trade, cannot possibly issue invoices to their customers, so there are a number of special retail schemes from which the one best suited to the business can be selected.

Small businesses, with the approval of Customs and Excise, may adopt the Cash Accounting Scheme which allows VAT to be accounted for on the basis of *payments* received and made rather than on *invoices* issued and received. The scheme has advantages and disadvantages. It is of particular benefit to those who have to give extended credit to customers, but those who are paid promptly may find themselves worse off under the scheme.

It provides auotmatic relief in respect of bad debts because VAT does not have to be accounted for if a customer fails to pay (under the usual system VAT on sales is paid to Customs and Excise as soon as the sales invoice is issued, without knowing whether that invoice will be paid).

From the previous chapters, which assume that the cash accounting scheme is not adopted, it will be seen that VAT is recorded automatically as the analysis books are filled in.

In the sales and purchases books VAT is separated from the 'goods' value of invoices and bills and, similarly, in the cash and bank books it is separated from all receipts and payments relating to 'cash' transactions – those sales and purchases which are not made on credit.

The total value of sales and purchases, and the VAT included in them, are instantly available when the books are added up at the end of each month. These figures are used to complete a VAT summary, as illustrated.

By completing a VAT summary each month it is possible to calculate how much is owed to Customs and Excise (or how much will be refunded by them). This is just another business debt, like money owed to suppliers.

Customs and Excise publish a large number of books and leaflets explaining the VAT rules and procedures. If in doubt ask the local VAT office for help.

VAT summary

Month	Month	Month	Total	Month	Month	Month	Total
£	£	£	£	£	£	£	£

Output Tax

Sales Cash Bank							

Input Tax

Purchases Cash Bank							

	Net Payable/ tax Receivable			Net Payable/ tax Receivable	

Sales (excluding VAT)

Sales Cash Bank							

Purchases (excluding VAT)

Purchases Cash Bank							

9. Distinguishing between capital and revenue receipts and expenditure

Capital and revenue expenditure

It is vital to understand the difference between the terms 'capital' and 'revenue.'

Capital Expenditure is that incurred in acquiring assets necessary for the business to be carried on, for example, land, buildings, plant, machinery, office equipment, motor vehicles. Such expenditure will include any installation costs and fees as well as the invoice price of each item. Capital expenditure is included as an asset on the balance sheet.

Revenue Expenditure is that incurred in actually carrying on the business: for example, rent, wages, insurance, purchase of raw materials or goods for resale etc. It will include repairs and maintenance of tangible assets and an annual charge for their depreciation. Revenue expenditure is deducted from sales income to produce the profit (or loss) for the year; that is, it is included in the profit and loss account. The importance of this distinction can best be illustrated by an example:

> A business buys a van so that it can save on delivery costs being incurred with transport contractors.
> The van will have a useful life to the business of four years.

To charge the whole cost of the van against the sales in the year of purchase would obviously distort the profit figure for that year and for the following three years – too much expense in the first year and none in the other three, although the van will still be used. The van is a tangible asset. Its cost must be added to the value of the 'Fixed Assets' of the business and, written off, (that is, included in calculating profit) over the four years of the van's expected life by charging depreciation of one quarter of the cost against the sales of each of the four years.

Example

A van purchased in 1992 for £2,000 has an estimated life of four years. The cost must be added to the value of fixed assets and depreciated, or written off, over the four years 1992 to 1995. This will have to be done by including in the revenue costs of each year, a charge equal to one quarter of the cost of the van and at the same time deducting the same amount from the value of the fixed assets.

Year	Original cost of van to be added to fixed assets (balance sheet)	Depreciation charged in the accounts each year (profit and loss account)	Written-down or book-value of the van at the year end (balance sheet)
1992	£2,000	£500	£1,500
1993		500	1,000
1994		500	500
1995		500	nil

The running costs of the van are revenue expenses, of course, and must be charged against sales income as they are incurred.

Difficulties often arise, for example, in deciding whether loose tools of a trade are tangible assets and should be treated as capital expenditure.

As a general guideline it may be helpful to use the rule that, to be a tangible asset, an item must:

increase the value of the property or assets of the business
have a useful life of at least two years

be readily identified at any time
and cost more than £100.

If these conditions are not met it is not advisable to include an item as a tangible asset.

For each fixed asset a depreciation charge has to be calculated to spread its cost over its useful ife. This is tedious when it comes to a large number of small items, many of which may be difficult to locate when the auditor has to take an inventory of fixed assets – in this case it may be sensible to charge the cost as revenue expenditure.

You must always be able to justify your classification of expenditure between capital and revenue because it will alter the profit for the year – the Inland Revenue may ask you for details of your classification. Obviously, the more expenditure that is classed as revenue, the more you will be charging against income for the year, the smaller your profit will be, and the less tax you will have to pay.

Clearly capital expenditure is made to provide the business with the facilities to enable it to operate now *and in the future* – not part of the day-to-day cost of running the business.

A fixed asset by its very nature, will wear out or become obsolete and have to be replaced. Account must be taken of this when assessing profit. This is the purpose of depreciation, which makes it possible to include in the costs of running the business a proportion of the cost of the asset each year, and aims to have included the whole cost of the asset by the end of its expected life.

An adjustment is made if the asset is sold, so that the actual cost to the business is the amount actually set against the profit over the asset's life.

Capital and revenue receipts

Money contributed or subscribed to the business and loans received from the bank (or loan funds, relatives or friends) is not trading income, but capital receipts.

Sometimes equipment is introduced by the proprietor or a partner. This is the introduction of 'capital in kind' instead of in money. The value of the equipment at the date when it is introduced can be added to the fixed assets and to the capital introduced by the person. It is not trading income – it is clearly capital.

Receipts from the sale of assets are not income, they are capital receipts. They must be set against the book value of the asset (the value which was added to 'Fixed Assets' when it was bought less the depreciation charged since its purchase). The difference between the book value and the price for which it is sold is treated as a profit or a loss on sale or disposal and this is included in the costs of running the business in that year.

In fact, the difference shows the extent to which the depreciation charged has been over- or under-stated.

Revenue receipts are solely the income which results from carrying on the business. Income from the sale of goods or work done are clearly revenue receipts. So are the proceeds from the sale of scrap, seconds or redundant stock because they relate to the running of the business.

Failure to make the proper distinction between capital and revenue income and expenditure will make any profit statement and balance sheet both inaccurate and misleading.

Example

Over the page is a draft profit statement and balance sheet prepared from the books of a company.

Profit statement for the period	
	£
Income from sales	40,000
Purchases of stock	20,000
Wages	10,000
Other expenses	14,000
Depreciation	1,000
Total costs	45,000
Profit or (loss)	(5,000)

Balance sheet	At beginning of period £	At end of period £
Stocks	4,500	4,000
Debtors	7,500	7,000
Cash at bank	3,500	1,500
Current Assets	15,500	12,500
Deduct		
Creditors	(1,500)	(2,500)
Net current assets	14,000	10,000
Fixed assets at book value	30,000	29,000
Total assets	44,000	39,000

Notice that the decrease in the value of total assets during the period equals the loss shown on the profit statement. This would be a true statement of the financial position if the capital expenditure has been correctly recorded.

But suppose that the £14,000 – 'other expenses' – includes £6,000 relating to the purchase of a lathe which has an estimated life of ten years. This should have been recorded as capital expenditure and added to the total value of fixed assets. Only a depreciation charge equal to one tenth of the cost (£600) should have been included with other expenses. This would make other expenses £8,000, depreciation £1,600 and total costs £39,600. The result would then be a profit of £400 instead of a loss of £5,000.

On the balance sheet, fixed assets would become £34,400 (£6000 cost less £600 depreciation added to fixed assets) making the total assets £44,400 thus showing an increase of £400 during the period – the profit.

Now suppose also that the £40,000 income from sales is found to include the receipt of £500 from the sale of a redundant drilling machine. This was purchased nine years ago at a cost of £3,000 and has been depreciated during this time at the rate of £300 each year so that it now has a book value of £300 – one year of its expected life remaining.

The £300 book value of the drill should have been deducted from the value of fixed assets because the drill no longer exists. The further £200 received can be said to be a profit. But perhaps more accurately, it shows that in writing down the book value of the drill to £300, the depreciation charge has been too much (it should have left a book value of £500 – the sales value) and this needs to be corrected by deducting the £200 'profit' from the charge for this year.

In this case, the correct income from sales was £39,500, the depreciation charge £1,400 (the new charge of £1,600 less £200) and the total costs £39,400 (£20,000 + 10,000 + 8,000 + 1,400). This will show the profit to be £100 (sales income £39,500 – costs £39,400).

On the balance sheet, fixed assets would be valued at £34,100 (the new fixed asset value less the book value of the drill) and the total assets at £44,100 thus showing an increase during the period of £100 – the profit.

The schedule overleaf shows how each of these corrections alters the position.

Profit statement for the period			Balance sheet at the end of the period		
	£	£			£
Income from sales	40,000		Stocks		4,000
Deduct: sale of drill	500		Debtors		7,000
		39,500	Cash at bank		1,500
			Current assets		12,500
			Deduct:		
Purchases of stock		20,000	Creditors		2,500
Wages		10,000			
Other Expenses	14,000				
Deduct: cost of lathe	6,000		Net current assets		10,000
		8,000			
Depreciation	1,000		Fixed assets	29,000	
Add: re: new lathe	600		*Add:* new lathe	6,000	
	1,600			35,000	
Deduct: profit on			*Deduct:*		
sale of drill	200		Book value of		
		1,400	drill sold		300
					34,700
Total costs		39,400	*Deduct:*		
			Depreciation		
			on new lathe		600
					34,100
Profit or (loss)		£100	Total assests		£44,100

See how the incorrect treatment of capital expenditure distorts the profit figure. In fact, in this example, the original draft showed a large loss, and the true result was a small profit.

Moreover, the value of the business was understated in the draft balance sheet because the total assets figure did not include the value of the newly purchased lathe.

10. Work timetable

Weekly jobs

	Cash book	Bank book	Sales book	Purchases book	Others
From the morning mail		Write cheques received on paying-in slip and pay into bank	Mark off cheques received against the invoices paid and re-file invoices in 'money received' file	Enter bills received from suppliers and file them in 'bills to pay'	
During the day	As they arise, record all receipts and payments in cash book in cash box	Write cheques to pay bills, wages, etc.		Mark off invoices as they are paid and re-file them in 'bills paid'	
At the end of day	Balance cash box and till. Bank takings...	complete paying-in slip and pay into bank	Enter invoices sent to customers and file them in 'money to collect'		

	Cash book	Bank book	Sales book	Purchases book	Others
Monday	Write up cash book for previous week from book in the cash box, balance it and to adjust float....	write cheque for cash or pay surplus into bank			
		Write up bank book from paying-in slips and cheque book stubs			
Wednesday				Prepare payroll of wages for work done in the previous week	

Monthly jobs

Week 1

1. Provisionally add up each column in each of the books for the previous month – cash, bank, sales, purchases – and make sure that the analysis columns cross cast to the total column.
2. Reconcile the bank book with the bank statement (Chapter 5). Correct the bank book for any overlooked direct debits etc.
3. Prepare overdue lists from the sales and purchases books (Chapter 6). Reconcile them:

Total of previous list
   Plus sales/purchases for the month
   Minus money received/paid as per cash/bank books
   Equals total of current list.

Correct the books as necessary.
4. Complete the adding up and cross-casting of each book.
5. Transfer the totals of the VAT columns from each book to the VAT summary.

Week 2

1. Complete the Inland Revenue payment book by entering details of PAYE, National Insurance, Statutory Sick Pay etc from the payrolls of the preceding tax period.
Send the completed slip to Inland Revenue, with a cheque, by the due date.
2. **Optional**
From the books, complete:
   Analysis of expenses
   Summary of income and expenditure
   Summary of assets.
3. **Optional**
Assess:
   Goods received but not invoiced
   Goods dispatched but not invoiced
   Prepayments
   Provisions
   Stocks
   Depreciation.
4. **Optional**
Complete profit and loss account and balance sheet.

Quarterly jobs

1. Add up the VAT summary for the VAT quarter.
2. Complete the VAT return and send it, with a cheque if necessary, to HM Customs and Excise.

11. Problem areas and special notes

Recording hire-purchase transactions

Finance agreements which provide for the ultimate transfer of the ownership of an asset from the finance company to the business need special accounting treatment. The following guidelines may assist.

The cost of an asset bought under a lease or hire-purchase agreement is made up of:

> The cash price (including VAT)
> *plus* the interest charge made by the finance company.

The total cost is then payable by equal instalments over the life of the agreement.

The cash price of the asset is added to the value of fixed assets just as it would be if the asset was being bought outright, but, because the agreement establishes the finance company as a creditor, the cash price is also added to a liability account called 'lease/HP creditor'.

The situation is really that the finance company has loaned the business the amount of the cash price and will charge interest on the loan until it is repaid.

As with other fixed-term loans, the capital repayments and the interest are calculated and spread equally over the term of the agreement.

Therefore each instalment that is paid is made up partly of a capital repayment of the loan and partly of the interest charged by the finance company.

The standing order by which each instalment is paid must be written in the bank book and analysed to columns headed 'lease/HP creditor' and 'HP interest'.

The repayment of the loan is a capital payment and is put under 'Lease/HP Creditor' while the interest element, being a revenue item, is put under 'HP Interest'.

Each month, if the capital payment under 'lease/HP creditor' is deducted from the amount originally established when the asset was bought, it will reveal the capital amount still owing to the finance company. By the end of the agreement the amount owing will be reduced to nil.

The revenue account – 'HP interest' – will be included, each month, in the costs of running the business.

Keep a record of all such agreements so that payments can be correctly analysed.

For example:

Cash price (capital cost)		£10,000
VAT		1,750
Interest		5,400
		17,150
Deposit paid – VAT	1,750	
Capital	1,000	
		2,750
Balance payable in		
36 instalments of £400		£14,400

Each instalment is therefore made up of:

Interest	5400/14400 x 400 =	150
Capital		250
		£400

Loan repayments

Money may be borrowed from a bank, a loan fund or some private source. Banks and loan funds usually make their loans for a fixed term which are repayable over, say, five or perhaps seven years.

Repayments are usually calculated to arrive at a constant monthly amount which includes varying proportions of capital repayment and interest.

Most lenders will request that the monthly repayments be made by standing order. Banks will often show the repayment of capital and interest separately on the bank statement. Loan funds will probably provide, at the outset, a schedule showing when each payment is due and how it is made up of capital and interest.

A loan is a capital receipt and must, therefore, be separately analysed in the bank book, that is, not in the same column as receipts from sales. When making an entry for the standing order, put the capital repayment in a column head 'loan'. This is a capital payment and must not be included with the business running costs.

But put the interest element, which is a revenue expense, in a column headed 'loan interest' and include it when assessing the running costs.

The treatment is very much like that of HP repayments described in the preceding paragraph.

Recording wages and PAYE

Every week, or every month, a payroll must be prepared.

It will show how each employee's gross wages (earnings before deduction of PAYE etc) are calculated. They may be a regular weekly or monthly sum or they may be based upon hours worked multiplied by an hourly rate, plus overtime, bonus etc.

The payroll will also show the deductions for PAYE and employee's National Insurance which have to be calculated by reference to Inland Revenue tables, and any other deductions such as pension contributions, savings or charitable donations.

The net pay – the amount to be paid to each employee – is then calculated by deducting PAYE etc from the gross wages.

Weekly paid employees are usually paid one week in arrears – that is wages earned up to one Friday are paid on the following Friday. Thus, there is always one week's pay owed by the business. This is the 'wages creditor' and represents the amount of net pay outstanding.

Similarly, deductions from wages, such as PAYE, are paid over during the following month and there is always a debt owed by the business to the Inland Revenue in respect of these items.

It is useful to keep a wages book, or a wages record, as a summary of the payroll and in particular, of the debts to employees and to the Inland Revenue.

Keep the record on a monthly basis using an analysis sheet having seven columns – one for each week's wages (there may be five weeks in a month), one for monthly wages and a total column.

Each week and each month enter the gross wages and the employer's National Insurance contribution. This makes up the total cost of wages to the business. Then enter the deductions – PAYE, employee's National Insurance and any others. Lastly, show the net pay – the gross wages minus the deductions.

When wages are paid, enter the cash or cheque in the cash book or bank book and mark off the payment on the wages record in the same way as bills are marked off in the purchases book. Likewise, mark off the deductions when they are paid over.

Wages or deductions not marked off at any time represent money owed by the business.

Because the cash or cheque paid out to employees is to settle a 'debt', the entry in the cash or bank book must be analysed to 'wages creditor' not wages. Similarly, the payment of the deductions must be analysed to PAYE or to 'deductions from wages', not to 'wages'.

Recording personal drawings

The directors of a limited company are employees and they are paid a salary which, in the same way as other employees, is subject to PAYE and employee's National Insurance. The proprietor or the partners of a business are not employees and they are not paid a 'wage' or 'salary'.

Technically, they have to wait until the end of the year when the accounts are prepared and the profit can be calculated; the profit belongs to them – it is their income. They can pay themselves as much, or as little, of it as they want – of course, assuming that the money is available and has not already been spent to buy more stock or is, perhaps, still owed to the business by its customers.

However, they are allowed to make 'drawings' each week or each month or whenever they wish. It must be appreciated that these drawings are really part of the profit being taken out in anticipation of its being available when the profit is eventually calculated at the year end.

A proprietor has only himself to think about and if he draws out too much he will either have to repay it or the business may become bankrupt. The same thing applies in the case of a partnership, except that more than one proprietor is involved. If one of the partners draws out more than his share he can be called upon to repay. If they all draw too much they may all have to repay.

By definition, drawings are part of the profit. They are *not* part of the running costs of the business.

Whether they are in cash from the till, from the cash box or cheques drawn from the bank, drawings must be analysed in the books to a separate column so that they can be excluded from the running costs of the business.

Sometimes they may be taken 'in kind' or by the business paying some personal expenses. For example, the business may buy petrol for the proprietor's wife's car or pay a home telephone bill. Such expenses must also be analysed to 'drawings', unless, of course, it can be demonstrated that the expenses were truly on behalf of the business.

Because they are not wages, neither PAYE nor National Insurance is deducted from drawings. Like self-employed people, proprietors and partners are not subject to PAYE. Instead, they pay income tax on the profit of the business which is calculated at the end of each year, before the deduction of the year's drawings, and they contribute National Insurance by a Class 2 stamp.

Technically, the sales income of the business (the money received from customers) is the proprietor's income, but there are certain allowable deductions which can be made from that income. In the main, the allowable expenses are those which were incurred 'wholly and exclusively' in the conduct of the business. The Inland Revenue can be very strict in the interpretation of the rules.

In a partnership, the profit is shared between the partners in whatever proportions they have agreed. Their share of the profit becomes their personal income for tax purposes. Of course, everyone has personal allowances under the Income Taxes Acts, and these are deducted from the income before tax is calculated.

It matters not whether the drawings are greater or less than the profit. If they are greater, it is presumed that some of the original cash put into the business as capital has been taken out. If they are less, it simply means that some of the profit has been left in the business ('ploughed back'). In either event, income tax is paid on the profit, not the drawings, and it is payable in equal instalments on 1 January and 1 July each year.

Accounts do not have to be made up to 5 April in each year. The business can decide the date of its year-end. The Inland Revenue will regard the profit of one accounting year as the income for the tax year beginning on the following 6 April.

There are special rules which apply to the first and last years of a business but, for example, if the business makes up accounts to December each year, the profit in the year to December 1990 becomes the income of the proprietor for the tax year 1991-92 and tax will be payable on 1 January and 1 July 1992.

Remember that income tax is not a business expense, it is a personal expense. If it happens to be paid by a business cheque, it is paid on behalf of the proprietor and must be analysed to his drawings in the bank book. It cannot be allowed as a business running cost.

The use of credit cards

For purchases

This is often seen as a convenient way of obtaining credit.

In reality it is equivalent to having a credit account with a supplier, but in this case, the 'supplier' is the credit card company from whom a monthly statement is received instead of from the suppliers from whom the goods were purchased.

Following this logic, treat every slip received when charging purchases to a credit card as if it were a supplier's bill. Give it a consecutive number, enter it in the purchases book and file it in the 'bills to pay' file.

The monthly statement from the credit card company is the same as a statement from a supplier. Check off the items on it against the slips and the purchases book. Select the bills to be paid and mark them off in the purchases book as the cheque is written.

If payment of a lump sum is made, treat it in the same way as any other such payment to a supplier.

If payment is not made by the due date the credit card company will charge interest. This interest should be recorded separately as when any supplier charges interest.

For sales

If the business accepts credit cards from customers, each slip issued is, in effect, an invoice to be paid later, not by the customer but by the credit card company.

The slips must be put into a separate file – one for each credit card company – and they must be sent off to the credit card company to claim payment according to the procedure laid down by individual credit card companies.

A record, kept separately from the sales book, will be needed to check on amounts owed to the business by the credit card companies. Try to use their documentation for this purpose. Mark off money received in the same way as other customers' cheques are marked off in the sales book. In the bank book, analyse the receipt to a separate column for 'credit companies', not to 'debtors'. This will help to check money owed by the credit card company, and with the preparation of the overdue list at the end of each month.

Settlement by the credit card companies may be made more promptly than it would have been by some customers, but the card company may make a charge. This charge will have to be treated as a 'discount allowed' but should be analysed separately so as not to confuse it with other discounts allowed to specific customers.

Appendices

The keeping of personal ledger accounts

A personal ledger (see page 74) can be particularly helpful if there are customers to whom more than one invoice is sent each month, or if there are suppliers from whom purchases are made more than once a month.

Although the state of each customer's and each supplier's account can be found from the sales book or the purchases book, or from the overdue lists, the process can be somewhat tedious when a fairly large number of invoices or bills is involved.

Personal ledgers can make the job easier in such circumstances.

A separate page in the ledger is set aside for each customer and on it is written the details of every invoice sent out and every payment received. The difference between the value of invoices and that of payments received is the amount owed by the customer. It is possible to relate the payments to individual invoices and ascertain those which are outstanding.

By this means the status of the account can be seen at a glance. At the end of each month the customer's sheet can be copied to become a statement of the account which can be sent to the customer to explain and remind him of the debt. An overdue list can be prepared by listing all the balances from the ledger.

A separate page can also be set aside for each supplier and on it can be written the details of all bills received and all payments made. This clearly shows the status of the account with each supplier.

It is also helpful if the supplier sends a statement which shows how he thinks the account stands. It is a simple matter to check the supplier's statement against the sheet in the ledger – obviously, they should be the same.

Ledgers can be used instead of the sales and purchase books, but remember that sales and purchase books are also needed to account for VAT, so some alternative has to be arranged. The alternative might be a ledger control account – a page on which is written the total value of all invoices sent out, showing the VAT included, and all money received. A check will have to be made to ensure that all the balances from the individual pages add up to the same total as the balance of the control account.

Of course, there needs to be one control account for customers and another for suppliers.

The use of ledgers is optional. It will be appreciated that they can be useful in many circumstances, and some people prefer to use them anyway. But it may be that, by the time ledgers become advantageous, the business will have grown sufficiently to consider using a computer program which will provide a ledger facility.

A simple form of management accounts

The cash and bank books, with the associated sales and purchases books, are the heart of any bookkeeping system.

In these books all the business income, all the expenses, all the assets and all the liabilities are recorded and analysed by simply following a few rules.

From these records, it is not difficult to summarise the figures in the form of, for example:
   a statement of income and expenditure (or a profit and loss account) and
   a statement of assets and liabilities (or a balance sheet).

This is the preparation of accounts.

The preparation of financial accounts becomes a rather technical matter because there are laws and guidelines on how accounts must be prepared and how information must be displayed, particularly in relation to the accounts of limited companies. It is a job for a qualified accountant. But it is a job made much easier for the accountant and cheaper for the business, if the starting point is a well kept set of books.

However since a business depends on income exceeding expenditure to make a living, it makes sense that, to be sure of success, a business should not wait for annual accounts to give a snap-shot view of its progress once each year.

By the time the accounts are prepared, they are probably up to six months out of date. It is then too late to take corrective action about last year's problems which have been overtaken by those of this year.

It is quite possible for any business to prepare, from its books, a simple form of management accounts.

Summary of income and expenditure

1. Write up an analysis of expenses by using an analysis sheet on which figures can be copied into separate columns for each book (cash, bank, purchases) (see page 75).

Code	Account	Bills received	Cash book	Bank book	Total	Year to date
201	Purchases					
211	Direct wages					
220	Carriage					
	Total					
	Overheads					
301	Indirect wages					
302	Salaries					
401	Consumable stores etc					

2. Complete the summary (page 75), compare the direct costs with the sales, consider the gross profit (or mark-up) and think of ways in which it might be improved.

3. Look carefully at the cost of wages and overheads, and look for ways in which economies might be made.
4. Study an analysis of sales and gross profit by product and by market and consider how a better performance may be achieved – whether by economies of buying, production or design, by better sales pricing or a better product mix of sales.

Summary of assets and liabilities (page 76)

1. Study the stocks of materials and of goods for sale. Are they at too high a level? Are they slow moving? Is too much money being tied up?
2. Take a good look at the debtors and see who should be chased for payment of their debts.
3. Look at the creditors. Are they being kept waiting too long for their money? Are the Inland Revenue and VAT payments up-to-date?
4. Consider the investment in the business:
   Stocks *plus* debtors *plus* cash
   minus creditors
   equals liquid assets (current assets)
   plus the book value of fixed assets
   equals total investment.
   (a) What about the liquidity? Ideally the figure for 'liquid assets' should be about one-half of the sum of the value of stocks, debtors and cash.
   (b) If the amount of the total investment were to be invested in, say, a building society or National Savings or equities on the stock market, how much would it earn? How much is the business profit? Is the business doing well?

Forecast of cash flow

If there is a list of debtors (customers who owe the business money) it will tell you what next month's intake of cash is likely to be. Knowing the order book, it is not difficult to forecast income for two more months.

A list of creditors (suppliers to whom the business owes money) will tell how much has to be paid out next month, and, knowing the cost of wages and overheads, it is not difficult to forecast expenditure for two more months.

So nobody need be suddenly hit by a cash flow crisis – there must have been at least three months' notice of any problem and during this time action could have been taken to avert, or at least minimise, the effect. See page 77 for a suggested format.

These summaries are not financial accounts, but they can be prepared without any professional knowledge or assistance. They are only approximate figures but they are good indicators. Something available now which is nearly accurate is much more useful than something more accurate in 12 months' time.

Such summaries should therefore be written up each month, or at least every three months, to give guidelines on the running of the business.

Personal Ledger

Name and address		Phone Fax Contact name Terms			Account number Page Credit limit			

Date	Ref	Details		Invoice	Payment		Balance	

Monthly totals	Jan/July	Feb/Aug	Mar/Sept	Apr/Oct	May/Nov	June/Dec

Summary of income and expenditure

Code	Account	Month 1	2	3	4	5	6	Total
	Income							
101	Sales							
109	Sundry sales							
	Total trading income							
	Direct costs							
201	Purchases							
	(Increase) Decrease in stocks							
211	Direct wages							
220	Carriage							
	Total							
	Gross profit							
	% on sales							
	Overheads							
301	Indirect wages							
302	Salaries							
303	Casual labour							
401/19	Expenses							
499	Depreciation							
	Total							
	Trading surplus							
501/4	Sundry income							
	Net surplus for the month							
	Proprietor's drawings							
	Profit retained in the business							
	Year to date							
	Sales							
	Gross profit							
	% on sales							
	Overheads							
	Trading surplus							
	Sundry income							
	Net surplus							
	Drawings							
	Retained profit							

Summary of assets and liabilities

Code	Account	At beginning of year	At end of month 1	2	3	4	5	6
610	Stocks Raw materials							
611	Work in progress							
612	Goods for sale							
	Total							
620	Debtors							
621	Prepayments							
630	Money at bank							
631	Office cash							
	Current assets							
701	Trade creditors							
702	Provisions							
710	HP creditor							
715	Loans repayable							
720	Wages creditor							
721	PAYE/NIC due for payment							
722	Deductions from wages							
730	VAT due for payment							
630	Bank overdraft							
	Liabilities							
	Surplus (deficiency) of current assets over liabilities							
	Fixed assets at cost							
801	Land and buildings							
802	Plant and machinery							
803	Motor vehicles							
804	Office equipment							
805	Furniture and fittings							
	Total original cost							
	Deduct:							
810	Depreciation to date							
	Net book value							
	Total assets							
	Profit (loss) for the year							

Cash flow forecast

Account	Month 1	2	3	4	5	6
Income						
Cash sales						
Debtors						
Own capital						
Loans						
Grants						
Total						
Expenditure						
Consumable stores						
Repairs and replacements						
Power, light and heat						
Advertising						
Travelling						
Printing and stationery						
Postage and telephones						
Wages						
PAYE/NIC						
Other deductions from wages						
Proprietor's drawings						
HP payments						
Loan repayments						
Bank interest						
Capital expenditure						
Total						
Surplus (deficiency) of income over expenditure						
for the month						
for the year to date						

Further reading from Kogan Page

The Blackstone Franks Guide to Creating Cash: 45 Essential Techniques to Improve Your Cash Flow
The Cash Collection Action Kit, Philip Gegan and Jane Harrison
Cashflow and Credit Management: A Daily Telegraph Guide, V Hawkes and K Slater
Controlling Cash Flow, David H Bangs
Debt Collection Made Easy, Peter Buckland
Do Your Own Bookkeeping, Max Pullen
Financial Management for the Small Business, 2nd edition, Colin Barrow
How to Understand the Financial Press, John Andrew
Understand Your Accounts, 3rd edition, A St John Price
Understanding Company Accounts: The Daily Telegraph Guide, 2nd edition, Bob Rothenberg and John Newman

Business Basics Series

Business Plans
Controlling Costs
Costing Made Easy
Pricing for Profit